The Seasons of Life

by
Purusha Jackson-Cox

AuthorHouse™
1663 Liberty Drive
Bloomington, IN 47403
www.authorhouse.com
Phone: 833-262-8899

Because of the dynamic nature of the Internet, any web addresses or links contained in
this book may have changed since publication and may no longer be valid. The views
expressed in this work are solely those of the author and do not necessarily reflect the views
of the publisher, and the publisher hereby disclaims any responsibility for them.

Any people depicted in stock imagery provided by Getty Images are models,
and such images are being used for illustrative purposes only.
Certain stock imagery © Getty Images.

This book is printed on acid-free paper.

ISBN: 978-1-4343-4030-6 (sc)
ISBN: 978-1-4772-0071-1 (e)

Library of Congress Control Number: 2008900856

Print information available on the last page.

Published by AuthorHouse 01/20/2022

authorHOUSE

For my GrandMothers,
Olva Jackson and Vitalis Browne!

"Bye Mom, Bye Dad", yelled Naomi waving cheerfully from the front door. She was at her grandmothers' home for the weekend and she was sure her Nana would have fun activities planned for them. She always did!

As she shut the door, she could hear Nana in the kitchen. She hurried towards the sounds.

"Hi Nana!"

"Hi Naomi! How are you?"

"I'm fine Nana. Are we baking today?" Naomi asked excitedly.

"Yes we are, Naomi and I'm glad you're here to help me," Nana replied cheerfully.

As they greased the baking pans and sifted flour, Naomi asked Nana about the seasons.

"Nana, it's getting very cold now and I'm learning in school about Spring, Summer, Autumn and Winter."

"Is it going to be winter again soon?"

"Oh baby, it sure is", said Nana.

"Let me put this bread in the oven and I'll come sit with you Naomi."

Naomi ran into the living room and climbed up on her favorite chair; a big overstuffed sofa. She sank comfortably between the pillows as she waited for Nana.

When Nana was finished in the kitchen, she took her apron off, washed her hands and joined Naomi on the sofa.

"The seasons of life remind me of the Stages of Life," began Nana.

"The Stages of Life? What do you mean?" enquired Naomi

"Well, to get to my age you first have to start off like your baby brother Samuel."

"Were you once a baby too Nana?"

"Oh sweetheart, Nana chuckled, everyone, including me, start off as a baby before they grow up."

"That's why the seasons remind me so much of life's stages."

"Spring is a young, vibrant season which starts all the seasons. Everything is brand new!

It reminds me of you and baby Sammy. The air is fresh, the flowers are bright and colorful and the grass looks like a thick green rug. Even the cool breeze kisses you daily, like you kiss me!

"I love Spring Nana, but tell me more. What about the other seasons?" piped Naomi.

"Well Summer comes on in, right after Spring and that's a wonderful season too."

"It's a fun time to go to the shore, have picnics, and visit the water and theme parks."

"During this time you have some really hot and cool weather, but it promises a lot of excitement!"

"This season reminds me of your Aunty Sarah, like summer, there's never a dull moment with her."

"She's fun to be around", squealed Naomi with joy.

"Autumn or fall as you call it comes after Summer. Your mom and dad just love this season because it's a cozy, romantic time."

"I love the colors of the leaves too Nana!"

"Me too darling, and it's a period where everyone and everything settles down in preparation for the next season. The animals, stock up on food, to prepare for the very cold days ahead. It's a good time to take long walks and watch the changes in the plants and trees; and I know you just love helping to rake up the leaves!

"I do, because I'm a good helper Nana."

"That's right baby, and the last season which I think represents me is Winter."

"Why do you think it represents you Nana?" Naomi asked.

Nana smiled thoughtfully and replied,

"It's a mature season; at the end of all the other seasons. You see baby, I've lived through the Spring, Summer, and Autumn period of my life and I'm living the Winter period now."

"Winter is a beautiful time. The snow decorates the leafless branches and covers the ground like a thick blanket. And it's such a still, restful season."

"Aaah..........I really enjoy wintertime," said Nana

"You always tell the best stories Nana," said Naomi.

"That's why I love coming to spend time with you!"

"Shush now child, Nana grinned, "and let's go check on the bread. I think it's just about ready."

She took hold of Naomi's hand and they walked together into the kitchen.

Printed in the United States
by Baker & Taylor Publisher Services